Big Coloring Book of Large Print
Color By Number Designs

By Lilt Kids Coloring Books

COLOR TEST PAGE

COLOR TEST PAGE

This book contains images from two of our bestselling books, and , for much less than the cost of buying them separately. Enjoy!

• COLORING TIPS •

1) Relax & Enjoy:
Coloring is good for stress relief, anxiety, depression, and so much more. There's no wrong way to color. You can do it while you watch television, listen to music, drink tea, or while you do nothing but focus on your coloring. Don't compare your finished product to anyone else's. You'll improve the longer you keep at it, and you probably won't love every single image you create. That's okay! If you are enjoying the journey, that's all that matters.

2) Choose the right tools:
Colored pencils, crayons, markers, oh my! What you choose to color with is a very personal choice. Visit LiltKids.com/tools for a rundown of our favorite brands. If you choose markers, we recommend you put a blank sheet of paper behind your page so that the colors don't run through onto the next image.

3) Color schemes:
Try out your colors in the test pages at the beginning of this book, and pick out some that might go well together. If you also google "color scheme", you will find an abundance of websites for inspiration.

4) Getting the pages out of your book:
Unfortunately, we don't yet have the ability to offer perforated pages in our books. However, you can find a tool called a page perforator on amazon.com for under $4, and turn any coloring book page into a perforated page!

5) Share your work:
We want to see what you color! So do our illustrators. Snap a photo and show us your work. Go to LiltKids.com, and click on the social media link of your choice: facebook, twitter, instagram, or pinterest.

Or email it to us and we'll share it for you!

LiltKidsColoring@gmail.com

Really, we want to see it.

We hope you enjoy this book!
If you do, please consider leaving a review on
Amazon.com, it really helps us out.

1	Red
2	Green
3	Blue
4	Yellow
5	Gold
6	Pink
7	Light Green
8	Light Blue
9	Deep Yellow
10	Brown
11	Dark Red
12	Dark Green
13	Dark Blue
14	Orange
15	Purple
16	Light Violet
17	Violet
18	Cyan
19	Magenta
20	Dark Purple

1	Red
2	Green
3	Blue
4	Yellow
5	Gold
6	Pink
7	Light Green
8	Light Blue
9	Deep Yellow
10	Brown
11	Dark Red
12	Dark Green
13	Dark Blue
14	Orange
15	Purple
16	Light Violet
17	Violet
18	Cyan
19	Magenta
20	Dark Purple

1	Red
2	Green
3	Blue
4	Yellow
5	Gold
6	Pink
7	Light Green
8	Light Blue
9	Deep Yellow
10	Brown
11	Dark Red
12	Dark Green
13	Dark Blue
14	Orange
15	Purple
16	Light Violet
17	Violet
18	Cyan
19	Magenta
20	Dark Purple

1	Red
2	Green
3	Blue
4	Yellow
5	Gold
6	Pink
7	Light Green
8	Light Blue
9	Deep Yellow
10	Brown
11	Dark Red
12	Dark Green
13	Dark Blue
14	Orange
15	Purple
16	Light Violet
17	Violet
18	Cyan
19	Magenta
20	Dark Purple

1	Red
2	Green
3	Blue
4	Yellow
5	Gold
6	Pink
7	Light Green
8	Light Blue
9	Deep Yellow
10	Brown
11	Dark Red
12	Dark Green
13	Dark Blue
14	Orange
15	Purple
16	Light Violet
17	Violet
18	Cyan
19	Magenta
20	Dark Purple

1	Red
2	Green
3	Blue
4	Yellow
5	Gold
6	Pink
7	Light Green
8	Light Blue
9	Deep Yellow
10	Brown
11	Dark Red
12	Dark Green
13	Dark Blue
14	Orange
15	Purple
16	Light Violet
17	Violet
18	Cyan
19	Magenta
20	Dark Purple

1	Red
2	Green
3	Blue
4	Yellow
5	Gold
6	Pink
7	Light Green
8	Light Blue
9	Deep Yellow
10	Brown
11	Dark Red
12	Dark Green
13	Dark Blue
14	Orange
15	Purple
16	Light Violet
17	Violet
18	Cyan
19	Magenta
20	Dark Purple

1	Red
2	Green
3	Blue
4	Yellow
5	Gold
6	Pink
7	Light Green
8	Light Blue
9	Deep Yellow
10	Brown
11	Dark Red
12	Dark Green
13	Dark Blue
14	Orange
15	Purple
16	Light Violet
17	Violet
18	Cyan
19	Magenta
20	Dark Purple

1	Red
2	Green
3	Blue
4	Yellow
5	Gold
6	Pink
7	Light Green
8	Light Blue
9	Deep Yellow
10	Brown
11	Dark Red
12	Dark Green
13	Dark Blue
14	Orange
15	Purple
16	Light Violet
17	Violet
18	Cyan
19	Magenta
20	Dark Purple

1	Red
2	Green
3	Blue
4	Yellow
5	Gold
6	Pink
7	Light Green
8	Light Blue
9	Deep Yellow
10	Brown
11	Dark Red
12	Dark Green
13	Dark Blue
14	Orange
15	Purple
16	Light Violet
17	Violet
18	Cyan
19	Magenta
20	Dark Purple

1	Red
2	Green
3	Blue
4	Yellow
5	Gold
6	Pink
7	Light Green
8	Light Blue
9	Deep Yellow
10	Brown
11	Dark Red
12	Dark Green
13	Dark Blue
14	Orange
15	Purple
16	Light Violet
17	Violet
18	Cyan
19	Magenta
20	Dark Purple

1	Red
2	Green
3	Blue
4	Yellow
5	Gold
6	Pink
7	Light Green
8	Light Blue
9	Deep Yellow
10	Brown
11	Dark Red
12	Dark Green
13	Dark Blue
14	Orange
15	Purple
16	Light Violet
17	Violet
18	Cyan
19	Magenta
20	Dark Purple

1	Red
2	Green
3	Blue
4	Yellow
5	Gold
6	Pink
7	Light Green
8	Light Blue
9	Deep Yellow
10	Brown
11	Dark Red
12	Dark Green
13	Dark Blue
14	Orange
15	Purple
16	Light Violet
17	Violet
18	Cyan
19	Magenta
20	Dark Purple

1	Red
2	Green
3	Blue
4	Yellow
5	Gold
6	Pink
7	Light Green
8	Light Blue
9	Deep Yellow
10	Brown
11	Dark Red
12	Dark Green
13	Dark Blue
14	Orange
15	Purple
16	Light Violet
17	Violet
18	Cyan
19	Magenta
20	Dark Purple

1	Red
2	Green
3	Blue
4	Yellow
5	Gold
6	Pink
7	Light Green
8	Light Blue
9	Deep Yellow
10	Brown
11	Dark Red
12	Dark Green
13	Dark Blue
14	Orange
15	Purple
16	Light Violet
17	Violet
18	Cyan
19	Magenta
20	Dark Purple

1	Red
2	Green
3	Blue
4	Yellow
5	Gold
6	Pink
7	Light Green
8	Light Blue
9	Deep Yellow
10	Brown
11	Dark Red
12	Dark Green
13	Dark Blue
14	Orange
15	Purple
16	Light Violet
17	Violet
18	Cyan
19	Magenta
20	Dark Purple

1	Red
2	Green
3	Blue
4	Yellow
5	Gold
6	Pink
7	Light Green
8	Light Blue
9	Deep Yellow
10	Brown
11	Dark Red
12	Dark Green
13	Dark Blue
14	Orange
15	Purple
16	Light Violet
17	Violet
18	Cyan
19	Magenta
20	Dark Purple

1	Red
2	Green
3	Blue
4	Yellow
5	Gold
6	Pink
7	Light Green
8	Light Blue
9	Deep Yellow
10	Brown
11	Dark Red
12	Dark Green
13	Dark Blue
14	Orange
15	Purple
16	Light Violet
17	Violet
18	Cyan
19	Magenta
20	Dark Purple

1	Red
2	Green
3	Blue
4	Yellow
5	Gold
6	Pink
7	Light Green
8	Light Blue
9	Deep Yellow
10	Brown
11	Dark Red
12	Dark Green
13	Dark Blue
14	Orange
15	Purple
16	Light Violet
17	Violet
18	Cyan
19	Magenta
20	Dark Purple

1	Red
2	Green
3	Blue
4	Yellow
5	Gold
6	Pink
7	Light Green
8	Light Blue
9	Deep Yellow
10	Brown
11	Dark Red
12	Dark Green
13	Dark Blue
14	Orange
15	Purple
16	Light Violet
17	Violet
18	Cyan
19	Magenta
20	Dark Purple

1	Red
2	Green
3	Blue
4	Yellow
5	Gold
6	Pink
7	Light Green
8	Light Blue
9	Deep Yellow
10	Brown
11	Dark Red
12	Dark Green
13	Dark Blue
14	Orange
15	Purple
16	Light Violet
17	Violet
18	Cyan
19	Magenta
20	Dark Purple

1	Red
2	Green
3	Blue
4	Yellow
5	Gold
6	Pink
7	Light Green
8	Light Blue
9	Deep Yellow
10	Brown
11	Dark Red
12	Dark Green
13	Dark Blue
14	Orange
15	Purple
16	Light Violet
17	Violet
18	Cyan
19	Magenta
20	Dark Purple

1	Red
2	Green
3	Blue
4	Yellow
5	Gold
6	Pink
7	Light Green
8	Light Blue
9	Deep Yellow
10	Brown
11	Dark Red
12	Dark Green
13	Dark Blue
14	Orange
15	Purple
16	Light Violet
17	Violet
18	Cyan
19	Magenta
20	Dark Purple

1	Red
2	Green
3	Blue
4	Yellow
5	Gold
6	Pink
7	Light Green
8	Light Blue
9	Deep Yellow
10	Brown
11	Dark Red
12	Dark Green
13	Dark Blue
14	Orange
15	Purple
16	Light Violet
17	Violet
18	Cyan
19	Magenta
20	Dark Purple

1	Red
2	Green
3	Blue
4	Yellow
5	Gold
6	Pink
7	Light Green
8	Light Blue
9	Deep Yellow
10	Brown
11	Dark Red
12	Dark Green
13	Dark Blue
14	Orange
15	Purple
16	Light Violet
17	Violet
18	Cyan
19	Magenta
20	Dark Purple

1	Red
2	Green
3	Blue
4	Yellow
5	Gold
6	Pink
7	Light Green
8	Light Blue
9	Deep Yellow
10	Brown
11	Dark Red
12	Dark Green
13	Dark Blue
14	Orange
15	Purple
16	Light Violet
17	Violet
18	Cyan
19	Magenta
20	Dark Purple

1	Red
2	Green
3	Blue
4	Yellow
5	Gold
6	Pink
7	Light Green
8	Light Blue
9	Deep Yellow
10	Brown
11	Dark Red
12	Dark Green
13	Dark Blue
14	Orange
15	Purple
16	Light Violet
17	Violet
18	Cyan
19	Magenta
20	Dark Purple

1	Red
2	Green
3	Blue
4	Yellow
5	Gold
6	Pink
7	Light Green
8	Light Blue
9	Deep Yellow
10	Brown
11	Dark Red
12	Dark Green
13	Dark Blue
14	Orange
15	Purple
16	Light Violet
17	Violet
18	Cyan
19	Magenta
20	Dark Purple

1	Red
2	Green
3	Blue
4	Yellow
5	Gold
6	Pink
7	Light Green
8	Light Blue
9	Deep Yellow
10	Brown
11	Dark Red
12	Dark Green
13	Dark Blue
14	Orange
15	Purple
16	Light Violet
17	Violet
18	Cyan
19	Magenta
20	Dark Purple

1	Red
2	Green
3	Blue
4	Yellow
5	Gold
6	Pink
7	Light Green
8	Light Blue
9	Deep Yellow
10	Brown
11	Dark Red
12	Dark Green
13	Dark Blue
14	Orange
15	Purple
16	Light Violet
17	Violet
18	Cyan
19	Magenta
20	Dark Purple

1	Red
2	Green
3	Blue
4	Yellow
5	Gold
6	Pink
7	Light Green
8	Light Blue
9	Deep Yellow
10	Brown
11	Dark Red
12	Dark Green
13	Dark Blue
14	Orange
15	Purple
16	Light Violet
17	Violet
18	Cyan
19	Magenta
20	Dark Purple

1	Red
2	Green
3	Blue
4	Yellow
5	Gold
6	Pink
7	Light Green
8	Light Blue
9	Deep Yellow
10	Brown
11	Dark Red
12	Dark Green
13	Dark Blue
14	Orange
15	Purple
16	Light Violet
17	Violet
18	Cyan
19	Magenta
20	Dark Purple

1	Red
2	Green
3	Blue
4	Yellow
5	Gold
6	Pink
7	Light Green
8	Light Blue
9	Deep Yellow
10	Brown
11	Dark Red
12	Dark Green
13	Dark Blue
14	Orange
15	Purple
16	Light Violet
17	Violet
18	Cyan
19	Magenta
20	Dark Purple

1	Red
2	Green
3	Blue
4	Yellow
5	Gold
6	Pink
7	Light Green
8	Light Blue
9	Deep Yellow
10	Brown
11	Dark Red
12	Dark Green
13	Dark Blue
14	Orange
15	Purple
16	Light Violet
17	Violet
18	Cyan
19	Magenta
20	Dark Purple

1	Red
2	Green
3	Blue
4	Yellow
5	Gold
6	Pink
7	Light Green
8	Light Blue
9	Deep Yellow
10	Brown
11	Dark Red
12	Dark Green
13	Dark Blue
14	Orange
15	Purple
16	Light Violet
17	Violet
18	Cyan
19	Magenta
20	Dark Purple

1	Red
2	Green
3	Blue
4	Yellow
5	Gold
6	Pink
7	Light Green
8	Light Blue
9	Deep Yellow
10	Brown
11	Dark Red
12	Dark Green
13	Dark Blue
14	Orange
15	Purple
16	Light Violet
17	Violet
18	Cyan
19	Magenta
20	Dark Purple

1	Red
2	Green
3	Blue
4	Yellow
5	Gold
6	Pink
7	Light Green
8	Light Blue
9	Deep Yellow
10	Brown
11	Dark Red
12	Dark Green
13	Dark Blue
14	Orange
15	Purple
16	Light Violet
17	Violet
18	Cyan
19	Magenta
20	Dark Purple

1	Red
2	Green
3	Blue
4	Yellow
5	Gold
6	Pink
7	Light Green
8	Light Blue
9	Deep Yellow
10	Brown
11	Dark Red
12	Dark Green
13	Dark Blue
14	Orange
15	Purple
16	Light Violet
17	Violet
18	Cyan
19	Magenta
20	Dark Purple

1	Red
2	Green
3	Blue
4	Yellow
5	Gold
6	Pink
7	Light Green
8	Light Blue
9	Deep Yellow
10	Brown
11	Dark Red
12	Dark Green
13	Dark Blue
14	Orange
15	Purple
16	Light Violet
17	Violet
18	Cyan
19	Magenta
20	Dark Purple

1	Red
2	Green
3	Blue
4	Yellow
5	Gold
6	Pink
7	Light Green
8	Light Blue
9	Deep Yellow
10	Brown
11	Dark Red
12	Dark Green
13	Dark Blue
14	Orange
15	Purple
16	Light Violet
17	Violet
18	Cyan
19	Magenta
20	Dark Purple

"Enjoy free bonus images from some of our best-loved coloring books on the next few pages."

Find our books on Amazon.

MAGIC IN THE GARDEN
The Whimsical Adult Coloring Book

MAGIC OCEAN ADVENTURE
Adult Coloring Book

COLORING INSPIRATIONAL QUOTES
The Uplifting Coloring Book For Adults

Every day is a good day

Coloring Inspirational Quotes:

The Uplifting Coloring Book For Adults

OCEAN FANTASY
Beautiful Mermaid Coloring Book For Adults & Children

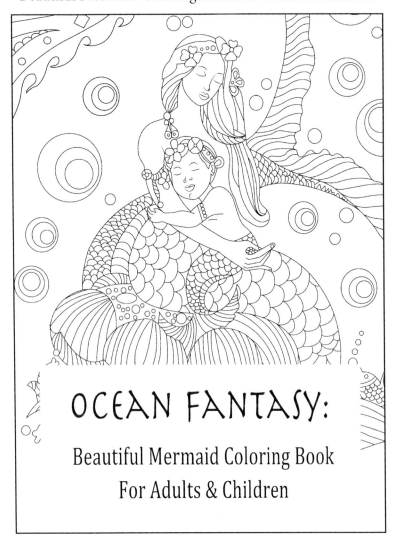

OCEAN FANTASY:

Beautiful Mermaid Coloring Book
For Adults & Children

IN MY ENGLISH GARDEN
Beautiful Illustrations For Adults Color

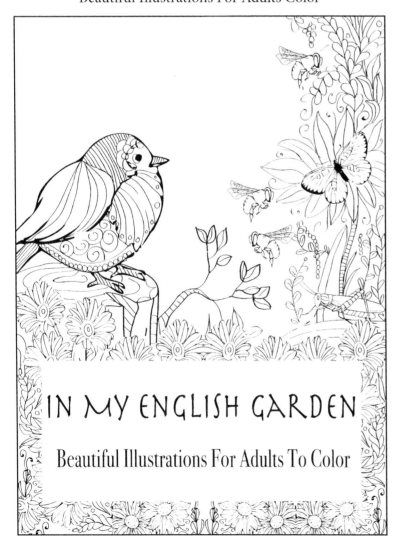

IN MY ENGLISH GARDEN

Beautiful Illustrations For Adults To Color

Animal Adult Coloring Book
Stress Relieving Patterns & Designs
Illustrated by Anastasiia Nikitina

Animal Adult Coloring Book
Nature Patterns for Creativity & Calm
Illustrated by Petya Kazantseva

Incredible India Coloring Book For Adults
Illustrated by Ananta Vishnu

Inspirational Quotes
A Positive & Uplifting
Adult Coloring Book
Illustrated by Mariya Stoyanova

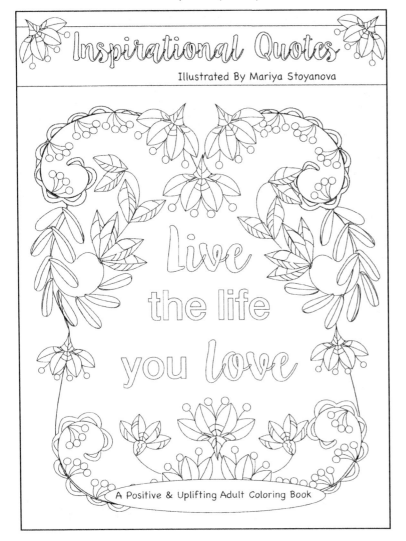

Cat Stress Relieving Designs & Patterns
Adult Coloring Book
Illustrated by Ananta Vishnu

This book comes with a free printable PDF version so you can print another one when you are done with this one!

Go to

LiltKids.com/download-60790

to download it.